Disclaimer

Dedication

This book is a dedication to and a prayer for Humanity and Democracy, the two of many essential social components for people to survive and develop as human beings with guiding lights, hope, and chances to have a life, learn to live, earn a living, and realize the values and meanings of life.

Acknowledgment

Human history inspires me to imagine the endless possible contexts in which a human may live and any person one may either autonomously choose or naturally socially get molded to be. The meanings of being and personal identity may emerge from individual comprehension of self, surrounding environments, and life-living experiences. Wars, racial prejudice and conflicts, human trafficking, bullying, and human abuse made me sad, tragic, puzzled, frustrated, challenged, and unsettled. However, empathy, compassion, love, hope, and positivity, the compelling sources of spiritual energy, drove me to write this book as a form of my prayer for genuine, unexhaustive human-helps-human efforts, decency, rapid intelligent actions, and mutual respect-and-compassion to be forever present in the world. The able humans who can help prevent and alleviate human tragedy and sufferance directly or indirectly despite imposing uncertainty and threats are unfading hope and heroes for all of us. Humanity, democracy, and the love for and from our families are potent inspirations for me to keep doing my best; this book is a part of it.

Contents

Introduction

A chance and capacity at an individual and a societal level to live and learn to discover personal potential, values, purposes, and choices in a lifetime are precious in human developmental processes along an unfolding fate toward life destination.

Liberty, Dignity, Freedom, Justice, Human Rights, and other elements of democracy may face arguments, threats, resistance, obstructions, distortion, contamination, and hidden limitations in real-life situations. Constructively, however, they serve as undeniable, powerful, inspirational, and impactful remedies for humans to thrive, live, and persevere in the interwoven self-societal developmental processes.

Human intelligence is a pool of seeds and nourishing nutrients for democracy. Reciprocally, democracy facilitates and enriches human intellectual and overall development. An ability to perceive, think, imagine, make decisions, and conduct oneself is vital for living and developing to one highest potential. An awareness of human souls' existence implies an individual intellectual capacity to recognize humanity.

Humanity is an empathetic divinity within human hearts, minds, souls, and spirits. It fortifies and facilitates expressions of love-kindness-and-compassion while distinguishing the differences between humans and nonhumans, including animals, robotic creatures, or material objects.

Everyone has biological parents to begin a life journey in the world. Having and living a life involves personal and social needs, including parental care, love, nutrition, guidance, education, and nurturing devotion to survive and develop from conception, birth, and childhood to reach maturity and individual life potential. The chance and quality of life depend on many factors, including genetics, natural and social environment, aspiration, courage, resources, circumstances, etc. Unfortunately, not everyone has a smooth and perfect pattern of life one may wish for. Metaphorically imagine plant seeds of the same species growing in different soils and weathers may yield diverse qualities of plants.

Life is not instantaneous magic emerging from a vacuum or nowhere; it is the sum of many components, changes and time, known and unknown, tangible and intangible, desirable and undesirable, and many other pros and cons or favoring and opposing forces. At any rate, one may examine life patterns and meanings through developmental perspectives. Be free to investigate the incredible reality of interconnected self-and-societal developments, which is always out there, naturally open for curiosity, observations, and intellectual introspection.

Democracy and humanity are mutually qualitatively inseparable and spiritually immeasurable. Both are divine building blocks of a remarkable human-made landscape for living a meaningful life and thriving through challenges along the life journey within the interwoven self-and-societal developmental processes. Unfortunately, many human contributing factors, such as ignorance, stupidity, ego, lust, greed, prejudice, hatred, insanity, pathetic attitudes, cruelty, terrorism, political conflicts, war, and crimes, can pollute and destroy such a landscape.

The superior advancement of human development compared to animals does not guarantee exceptional human behaviors under stressful competitions for limited resources, power contests for domination, conflict of interest, mental illness, blind ego, urge, hunger, greed, and life-threatening situations or insecurity.

People's involvement in democracy and humanity with variations of social debates about and inquiries for peace, freedom, education, justice, safety, and quality of life are practical implications of the constitution and civilization of the nation. However, chaotic events at various levels and locations are wake-up calls for more awareness that humanity and democracy need recognition, appreciation, promotion, preservation, adaptation, evolution, and 24/7 cooperative guardian actions from people who live under the umbrellas of social systems to preserve and enrich the opportunities to live, freedom to think, and much more. Like the heartbeats, humanity and democracy are vital social components or indispensable human assets, hope, companions of life, and shining light for living.

A life comprehension beyond blaming, complaining, criticizing, and judging anyone may lead to a profound understanding of the reciprocal relations between humans and sociopolitical systems in the natural world, which may lead to the discovery of more ideas for constructive resolution and prevention of human tragedies.

This book employs an aesthetic approach with a mixture of mandalas, poems, and reflections of life and professional experiences to emphasize the values, strength, and vulnerability of democracy, human social relations, and various aspects of undesirable social systems' influences upon humans. Most of all, it is imperative to continue to improve the ideas regarding how humans can come together to promote the quality of life and sociopolitical systems to make the world a better, safer, and long-lasting place for living, developing, balancing progress, and decent coexistence. Persevering navigation of collective intelligence, spirits, attention, relevant dialogues, practical debates, and proper actions may reveal and validate possible practical strategies to improve democratic systems in various dimensions.

Under The Light Of Freedom

The Freedom to live, learn, and think is a shining light for humans to envision life's values and possibilities. The Freedom and vision on the foundation of accessible education and its application can pave the way for further intellectual development in limitless fashions. Promotions of intellectual and overall human development per an avenue of Freedom are a noble strength of democracy, as anyone may examine its contents and countless life stories. Under the light of Freedom, one may define the true meanings of Freedom as one learns to free one's mind along the lines of social and natural limitations. Eventually, one may learn about Freedom's practical values and implications individually and socially with humility, humanity, creativity, passion, and innovation.

Democracy, human intelligence, and humanity are priceless assets for society and humans. In a moment of silence, anyone may wonder what else is more precious than the ability to realize and comprehend the being and existence of oneself in a world filled with energy, mysteries, possibilities, and adventures. The need for life ingredients and mobility may lead to an essential sense of broad social relations through the connectivity of kindness, caring, compassion, respect, appreciation, cooperation, exchanges, and trade. It is great to be free. Whatever, wherever, whenever, and however, it is never too late to realize and appreciate the value of empathy and mutual respect. They are virtuous bridges for civility and courteous socialization. Freedom allows possibilities, hope, wondering questions, cognition, imagination, cooperation, and evolution; Freedom unleashes creativity, productivity, and innovation.

An ability to know, differentiate, and choose between right and wrong is a foundation for self-discipline and aspiration for life construction and motions of living. Interactive self-and-social disciplines and development may suggest how humans influence each other on a social and natural platform. Generally, humans can think but may not choose to do so. Moreover, thinking styles may contrast; neither be similar nor the same. Among all these, morality is a divine result of intellectual development on worldly life living landscape, a quality component of humanity and democracy. Freedom to develop and evolve excellently is much more than just a wonderful thing.

Freedom allows anyone to imagine the parallel linkages between autonomously disciplined human beings and civil societies. One may envision them metaphorically in a colorful image of mutual reflections between self and society, like a prism. Humans may illuminate these spectacular reflective images per intellectual and spiritual development along their life trajectories. Under the light of Freedom, personally and socially, humans must work together to consciously own the Freedom to protect, preserve, and enrich human development, humanity, and democracy for the civility and peaceful coexistence of the human species. Understanding the potential, limitations, implications, and application of Freedom can make life interesting, fruitful, hopeful, and enjoyable.

Life In The Social, Symbolic, and Natural Context

Natural and human-made reality seem infinite as ongoing changes happen and time keeps moving forward. Nobody knows it all. What is going on? Where, when, why, why, and why can't we make the world safer, more hopeful, and even better as we develop with time? Changes are challenges for humans to comprehend, overcome, and thrive through regardless of what forms they may appear to be: hot or cold, positive or negative, constructions, destruction, progress or regress, lies, deception, misinformation, confusion, pain-and-sufferance, illusion, depression, ecstasy, misery, and so on. Changes are unstoppable and powerful realities. Changes may be good or bad; however, naturally, we prefer the better or the best for comfort, pleasure, security, serenity, longevity, and hope.

All kinds of threats to human existence seem so loud, powerful, cruel, dangerous, deadly, intimidating, humiliating, and overwhelming compared to humans' divine efforts to overcome them. Demands on comprehension about changes and what humans can do about them are endless invigorators for human struggles to live a life in society. Moreover, the complexity and threats of the changes are relentless challenges that can make life difficult, miserable, or unbearable for many. Fortunately, somehow, love, kindness, morality, compassion, intelligence, connection, and cooperation are powerful leverage in overcoming challenges and obstacles to improve and preserve the world from generation to generation.

Everything is happening on earth and everywhere, illuminating reality with many problems, pros and cons, ambiguity, haunted mysteries, uncertainty, fear, and hidden hope that seems to continue forever here and there. However, whenever we cannot find hope, we must create at least one, a very inspirational one, to live our lives wherever we do not have choices and there seems to be no fun. Spiritually, minds with morality, good intentions, and perseverance may lead the hopeless and helpless to meet human kindness, intellect, compassion, and cooperation for practical solutions and contributions.

What should humans do to acquire and live a long-happy-and-meaningful life? Confusion, frustration, fear, anger, anxiety, sadness, and hatred are neither solutions nor plans. Keep calm, and hang in there; together, we can bear and beat the challenges and evolve more than anyone may do them alone. Positivity, self-confidence, believing in mental strength, wisdom, courage, and hope may energize many people to keep thriving and never give up. Doing as best as possible may be a doable adaptive plan; do it as you can. Collectively and relentlessly, love, kindness, compassion, gratification, cooperation, and many more divine virtues can unite humans to overcome life challenges and adversaries.

The intangibility of the mind, intellectual capacities, hidden behaviors, and the unpredictability of changes in interactive reality are overwhelming for a human to embrace and comprehend alone. However, dynamic-systems-thinking, access to relevant information or knowledge, compassion, connections, and navigation of visionary intelligence may lead to possibilities, courage, and confidence to keep busy living with meaningful purposes. Eventually, in thriving to live and make one best, synergistic application of all available intelligence, transparency, effective communications, and cooperative actions may reveal pathways and priceless tools to overcome predicaments, obstacles, and adversaries from anything anywhere, including natural disasters and the negative behaviors of syndical self-centered fools and tyranny.

Life in social, symbolic, and natural environments may be complex, mysterious, unpredictable, and hard to comprehend. Nevertheless, human behaviors, symbols, languages, communications, uncountable inventions, and constructions are examples of human creativity, a tiny part of reality, in a natural-universal context of endless mystery and complexity. They are the pieces of evidence of living, being, many incredible things humans can do, and the enduring existence of the human species.

However, regardless of any potential or limitation, a reasonable thing to do is to be strong and wise; we shall not live with fear but instead with hope, courage, relentless best effort, boundless imagination, and wisdom light.

A combination of awareness, good intentions, an open mind to learn, and an indomitable will to live through all the challenges by always doing one best seems to be the best bet for a meaningful life. Get set, beware, and be motivated; a decent mind and self-discipline with logical expectations can be a leading run crunching for success. Refusal to give up while trying to learn, comprehend, adapt, and evolve parallels a skillful pole jumping aiming high to fetch the abundant unbeatable spiritual energy of being within the moment of autonomous soul energy transformation and evolution.

Oneness and Wholeness

Instinct and intellectual development toward self-preservation, surviving, and living a given life are essential ingredients for existence in addition to the functional biophysical structures of any living system ranging from a primitive cellular level to more and more complex animal and human levels. Humans are much more sophisticated and advanced than other living things or animals. With ordinary senses in any situation, humans may examine and learn about humans along the pathway of living and being. It is a worthy endeavor for humans to learn about themselves and others and eventually discover sensible things to do for survival, existence, and progress at personal and societal levels.

In any case, everyone is unique overall; getting busy living may be parallel with keeping on doing one best. While doing one best, respect and appreciation of the values of life may invite humanity, empathy, practical cooperation, and many more humans' best for peaceful living and civilization.

Focusing on a personal level, living a given life requires instinct, an individualized self-serving ability, adaptability to live, and creativity to evolve. All these qualities may supposedly improve per developmental processes and education. No matter how far one may develop, reach out, or climb up toward life achievement, no one should claim the power or superiority to tamper or take such life-living potentials, chances, and capacities to live in society away from anyone. Everyone has the soul within the impermanent biophysical complexion under the natural law of energy manifestation and transformation. Human interactions are co-motions of living that may be harmonious, conflictual, constructive, destructive, or any outcome depending on various factors, including intellectual developments, beliefs, values, communications, and many hidden or unfolding reasons.

Infant crying voices are initial natural requests for food, love, comfort, and security. As humans develop, the voices for living a given life and being a human develop, transform, and display in uncountable fashions. Unfortunately, many million humans suffer silently, crying and dying alone per ongoing natural and chaotic sociopolitical events. Their voices vanish in the dispersing waves of undelivered messages, helplessness, misery, and mystery. In contrast, most of the rest may take their fortunes and self-proclaimed superiority over others for granted, enjoying luck, complaining, and blaming others when stuck in trouble. Small numbers of the world's population are well-educated and have leadership skills. How should the able minority lift and push the world forward with possible strength, wisdom, knowledge, skills, and whatever is available?

At a personal level, upbringing habits and behaviors from childhood may continue to the formation of adulthood hidden characters that affect job performance, surrounding people, social integration, and social systems to various extents. Generally, appropriate behaviors are complementary, whereas bullying and dangerous or destructive ones are undesirable and unsustainable to other humans and society.

The defenses against undesirable behaviors at personal and societal levels may be parallel but not necessarily the same. However, the events at those levels are human-made; struggles to live with continuous adaptations and evolutions for comfort, security, and hope are inevitable in interwoven self-societal developments. Life goes on, and so do the ongoing challenges. Mastering living skills is a compelling force to overcome fear with a cheerful attitude, courage, and mindfulness to thrive.

Realistically, neutralizing measures or perfect defenses against the challenges may be desirable. However, no one should take it for granted as the final or forever done deal settlement because of the continuity of changes naturally socially and the complexity of interwoven self-society developments. Wars, crimes, and human abuses are unfortunate breaking out challenges along human interactions in the fabrics of self-societal developmental processes. These problematic issues require humans' best efforts in every area to recognize and energize themselves to find solutions dynamically in continuously adaptive evolutionary fashions.

Prejudice and corruption can tamper, obscure, and obstruct humanity and many divine components of life. Availability and connectivity of compassion and collective intelligence at any moment of life are valuable and powerful resources for human-and-societal developments from various perspectives. Cultivations of oneness-and-wholeness chains of life connections on the platforms of human intellectual development may offer leading lights of empathy for humans to consider sensible cooperative living and divinity of being over destructive competitions, hatred, cruelty, jealousy, inhumane possessions, oppression, alienation, corruption, and prejudice against the difference.

Simple Chains Of Life-Living Economy In Democracy

On any occasion, "human-serves-human" links the chains of demand and supply in the economy of living, combining nature-made and human-made themes of life from birth, living, life enduring, and dying. Where may humanity, civility, and democracy fit in? Sociopolitical systems are human-made tools to manage and influence human behaviors and attain social orders under the power of system organizations, rules, laws, regulations, and leadership. Their complexity and sophistication require time, scholarly intelligence, and elite opportunities to comprehend deeply. Meanwhile, mediocrity may habituate in social flows, be busy with life struggles, or ignorantly pass by.

Based on the accumulative world history and human experiences, there is no perfect system to offer utopian or romantic quality services for everyone to live eternally and be forever happy and peaceful. Whatever may be, democracy provides the most people-oriented sociopolitical approach, as freedom, dignity, liberty, justice, and human rights are its fundamental values. It allows the people to interpret and apply the democratic system philosophy through the freedom to vote, self-expression, autonomy to be oneself, and many other sociopolitical activities. The blessing from humanity and democracy is immeasurable as they are earnest endeavors and contributing factors to incredible life-living landscapes where humans may continuously develop and cultivate the progress and benefits of the social systems.

Among all kinds of human interactions, including exchanges, trading, and competitions, democracy has tremendous implications for bringing out people's best along personal-and-societal developmental processes and multifaceted changes. It is undeniable that humanity is an embedded value and guiding light in the meanings and functions of "the system of the people, by the people for the people." Civility is a product of the progress of personal-and-societal development. However, it does not include dysfunctional behaviors and painful struggles in the processes.

People may interact, care, share, or exchange resources and behave according to their capacities and development levels under natural and human-made laws. The spectrums of human interactions constitute consequential social phenomena that reciprocally affect human lives in uncountable perspectives from a personal level to international levels. Nobody knows everything and can do everything on the pathways or processes of one life living; however, individual capacity and character may be unique within the scope of human potential and limitation. Freedom and chains of human interdependence and interactions in democratic systems offer more offensive-defensive protections and enrichments for intellectual development and overall human-and-societal developments than suppressive-abusive systems of dictatorships and autocracy of power monopoly.

The precious light of the human developmental potential to be oneself and live one life is an inborn gift everyone has that should shine throughout life. From a developmental perspective, humans should be intelligent enough to embrace self-and-other coexistence in a cooperative-constructive fashion or develop in that direction. Under the sky of nature, pinpointing to human societies, humans depend on or are affected by other humans directly or indirectly on the sociopolitical platform. The platform arises from accumulative outcomes of human interactions, social structures, cultures, locations, situations, communication, mobility, personal-and-social identity, etc. However, uniqueness belongs to the individual – no one can be you for you, or no one can be I for me. Individual active participation in self-and-societal development and life-living through education and democracy may alleviate the burden on the "systems of the people, by the people, for the people" and others in the systems. These are prominent values of democracy created by humans, humanity, and other human-divine qualities. The goodness from constructive intelligence and spirits, humanity, the divinity of being, education, active social participation, cooperation, and transparency make democracy solid, resilient, and valuable in meaningful-and-hopeful societies.

Energy, Time, and Human Beings

Energy and time are powerful, inferable components of actively functional systems ranging from galaxy and solar systems to living systems of endless mystery and complexity. Signals of existence may include but are not limited to forms, formlessness, activities, connectivity, and changes; these may or may not be detectable by humans. Based on humans' senses of perception, intuition, and imagination about reality, energy is intangible until it manifests in or transforms into tangible forms. To avoid getting lost in the mysteries of energy and time, one may narrow them down into a perspective of life living and being a human in earthbound habitats. Meanwhile, allow science and scientists to work on and be the sources of the information and facts to satisfy and answer any more profound curiosity, scrutiny, and wondering questions.

Struggles to live and thrive at one best are endless human endeavors in the world where everything keeps on changing under the natural law of energy manifestation and transformation in uncountable styles, levels, and speeds. Most living things and many humans may not pay attention to, beware of, or be able to comprehend these perspectives. Occasionally, anyone may realize that some things happen but never be able to understand the events in complete detail or put the actual reality on hold for later examination. Changes involve the dynamics of energy manifestation and transformation from the intangible to the tangible or vice versa. They are unstoppable, unextinguishable natural events like spinning earth, gravity, energy dynamics, momentum, sunshine, night, and day.

Along with changes, **time** is a tremendous human discovery of an immaterial reality that can catch human perception by using objective indicators in various forms and designs of the clock or watch such as a sand clock, wall clock, digital clock, wristwatch, etc. Relatively to sunrise-and-sunset and available instrumental capacities, we count time in milliseconds, seconds, minutes, hours, day, night, AM, PM, months, years, decades, century, etc. Clock time is an ordinary time that enormously influences humans' comprehension of reality and daily life. However, some may not understand or choose to ignore the meanings and values of the time. Changes reveal time. Meanwhile, time helps humans learn about changes and the implications of both the changes and time in various perspectives, dimensions, and directions.

Time, Time, and Time

Time, time, and time, Hm! Your time, my time, our time, human time, dog time, cat time, bird time, turtle time, good time, bad time, wrong time, lifetime, long time, short time, timeline, past time, future time, nap time, playtime, quality time, and wow! Whatever time, what is the time? Oh! What a time to think about time. How many times must one think about all of these to understand time? The answer is personalized; one may have to find time or make time to learn about time. There is no time limit; time is open, neutral, and has no prejudice or discrimination. Changes and time are always around us or with us. One may freely manage and allocate personal time. No discrimination; anyone is always welcome to learn and enable oneself to understand the meaning of time.

Time always accompanies ongoing changes and human-made rules using tools, instruments, and symbols to recognize and mark the time. Time is a visionary asset that can link to everything if one knows the surrounding environments and can recognize and analyze relevant information and facts. Hmm! Is it a confusing time, a time to act, or a wake-up time? Please, please repeat one more time about the real meaning of time. Well! Time is magic and active; time is a precious reflection of all kinds of changes while moving along with them, including children growing up and seasonal changes like fall, winter, spring, summer, and so on. Anyone may pay attention and learn about time on any occasion. For many, it may be a prime time to live a meaningful life and comprehend all kinds of time. Keep calm and disciplined; be kind and wise, no matter where or what time. Life always has a bright side with time.

Again, can anyone process and preserve time? Imagination is a route to find the answers. Regardless of any story that happened once upon a time, someone may wonder, feel sad, or delightfully have fun dancing with time. Time and again, humans have difficulty keeping up with challenges that continuously evolve with time. Connectivity of mutually re-enforceable human spiritual intelligence may amplify community capacities to rise and move forward ahead of time. Be impressed but not surprised; we all may rise and shine while moving with time.

Time is natural, bold, neutral, undiscriminating, unfolding, valuable, free, powerful, and never waiting for anyone. It is an incredible tool to guide our lives, and anyone may give oneself a high five when understanding the meaning and use of time.

Well! Do you believe in time (and taxes)? There are income taxes, sales taxes, transfer taxes, many other kinds of taxes, and tax time. However, there has been no time, compassion, or love tax so far. Be happy; there is time to enjoy nontaxable items such as good mood, smiles, and food. Well! Again, there is one interesting problem: it may be hard to figure out funny or grumpy taxes and count them out for happiness. Convincingly, however, the people who may be fans of or love tax are tax collectors and tax spenders. Busy or not, better or worse, never forget to pay taxes. Relax; take a deep breath and let go, somehow, taxes always accompany everyone on the road to the future.

As anyone may want to move to the future, in a hurry or not, at any level or style, time will take you there. One may imagine riding on a magic carpet, hopping and flowing over the clouds and rainbows on the way to the future along with time. Generally, humans may enrich themselves with time, mindful time, and tax-free time. Whatever it may be, there is plenty of time to think about time, and it is OK to love a peaceful time.

These may be inspiring or confusing puzzles about taxes and time. However, in any situation, many people may *not* want to think about time or taxes and keep doing their best, busy living until the end of their lifetime. Nevertheless, time may be a magical asset if one can conceptualize, apply, and navigate personal living time by living creatively, adaptively, and decently with all kinds of changes ahead of time. Time may be a precious gift to realize at all times.

An Earthbound Soul Landing

"Born to live" should be a synergy to "born to be a human being" in life viable motions for divine possibilities and evolving fate. The blissful soul energy inside a human body is the central light of life and being.

To live and to be must include being free to think. The freedom to think is a bright and hopeful light to start a life and self-development. It does not matter whether high, low, fast, or slow in terms of developmental level, style, and speed if they do not adversely affect anyone. Moment by moment, we gradually face the reality of life without expecting how hard or hurtful feelings may turn out to be when facing cruelty or merciless challenges while feeling happy and delighted with the light of love, kindness, and compassion.

An ability to think well and do well is a ringing bell for a joyful life journey, as one needs to manage one mind and emotions with or without coaching or education.

Experiences may teach us countless meanings of being and living when we portray various roles, alone or with others, in the scene of hot or cold weather, flood, fire, earthquake, war, peace, violence, and an incredible challenge. Hope, vision, good intentions, caution, and discipline may lead us to a high moral elevation and feel fine while pursuing a purposeful living.

Rapidly advancing technology and internet access to information, news, and knowledge have tremendously increased human chances to learn and live. However, inadequate or lack of guarantee for a valid proof of evidence, effective information filtration, and truth or fact validation confuses and misleads millions of humans in the wilderness of boundless information.

When examining destructive influences, aggressive intimidation, bullying, violence, and lies, anyone may wonder why certain humans behave destructively, inhumanely, or deceitfully. However, at least, routinely or occasionally, we may pray for goodness to prevail and keep on doing our best. Love, kindness, and compassion bless everyone anywhere in heaven or hell. They are great, free, and accessible virtues for humans to cultivate anytime, even during running, walking, dancing, cooking, eating, laughing, or crying. Spiritually and intellectually, one may fortify them from the mind inside. Understanding oneself and others requires time to comprehend human nature in isolation and community formation.

Per intuitive inference from personal experiences and meditation, soul energy may be inferable as the energy of being. Referring consciously or unconsciously to many sources one may encounter, the soul energy – the energy of being exists. One may not dictate, control, or choose the wholeness of a life journey or fate. Still, sincere, faithful, or good intentions can be powerful drives for one's actions or behaviors in daily living. Reality contains uncountable consequential events, activities, and interactions. Consequential daily motions of living done by humans imply that everyone is the driver of and should take responsibility for one's actions and outcomes in one life journey or unfolding fate. Everyone is a critical and indispensable part of the wholeness of one life. A little power can be a potent-and-divine one when one thrives on living and never gives up on doing one best. One accompanies oneself 24/7, anytime, good or bad, and is the ultimate personalized hero. Soul innately accompanies one awareness, cognition, will, feelings, and decision-making. It resides inside a person's body throughout a lifetime; it is precious but too mysterious to comprehend and define completely. Under a spiritual light, life is like a journey of a soul.

Soul, soul, and soul, yes, I agree, every human has a soul; close your eyes in a quiet, private, and safe environment, then take a deep breath, and be calm – you may touch and feel your skin and body with your hands. In contrast, your mind may feel the self and soul spiritually and deeply. The existence and boundaries of self and soul are precious to realize in a personal journey through life's trajectory in the eventful human world. It may take a critical moment or a lifetime to discover the freedom from internal and external influences that oppress or suppress a self-and-soul discovery and personal development. Self and soul awareness may be the key to living a complete life which may not perfectly fit any standard but fall into a divine way of being. A dignified soul is an invincible soul – an inferable core of being.

Education, Education, and Education

Education is a foundation for earning and living a meaningful life. It is an essential ingredient for human development as well as societal development. The quality of the people is the quality of the society; competent people mean a capable community and a viable nation. Quality education may inspire humans to choose a valuable pathway and actions to be a better human today than yesterday, develop and advance, if not much, it can be little by little in moving forward to a hopeful future.

Education is a wonderful gift humans may give to humans in various ways, academically or nonacademically, formally or informally, and so on. An infusion of a lifelong learning interest and inspiration to apply knowledge constructively is an indispensable component of education. Education is supposed to stimulate, promote, and nurture intellectual development and enrich other life features for one to be a well-rounded, decent human being and a competent member of society. Education is a lifelong endeavor and a success multiplier.

Never forget that qualified people mean a capable nation or affluent society; intellectual suppression, exploitation of the innocent and unsuspecting, oppression, and human rights violations are poisonous to the victims, the society, the country, and the world community. Education and training provide opportunities for acquiring social-and-living skills. Still, the action, practice, and application of the knowledge and skills at a personal level are at the discretion of the individual. Encouragement and advocacy for aspiration, self-discipline, and perseverance may facilitate personal development beyond the academic environment, extending to the real world's challenging landscape. Education is a powerful light to rescue, direct, save, and enrich human lives.

A synergistic alignment of competent leaders from everywhere can orchestrate decent human societies, from a private to an international or global level. Humanity and mutual respect may guide life values in preventing abusive and destructive behaviors. People are living components of social systems of various types, politically, economically, culturally, academically, etc. Humans design social systems, rules, regulations, provisions, policies, and many other social measures for social orders, behavioral control, disciplines, sustainable-and-functional society, etc. These perspectives involve behavioral science, which is beyond the scope of this book. However, anyone may take a look, listen, and learn how an individual can influence others and society and reciprocally the other way around by paying attention, wondering, and applying common sense and logical thinking to comprehend human behaviors routinely. Education is essential in self-and-societal development and empowerment.

Lay persons may not have formally high-level, institutionally bound education; curiosity and interest can naturally lead to awareness, wonder, ambition, and observation. Personal interests, experiences, and independent hedonic thinking habits may help one develop and sharpen personal critical thinking skills. All these, with good intentions, moral capacity, and constructive dialogues, may lead to developing and communicating new ideas and information in the community, nation, and global society. Once the good ideas reach capable-powerful leadership, constructive changes or improvements in related matters may occur.

Education, humanity, and democracy are priceless divine social gifts people can cultivate, fortify, preserve, and give to each other in adorable manners. They have incredible potential to inspire, facilitate, and enrich valuable idea generation, decent behaviors, and intellectual endeavors for constructive changes and life improvement from personal to societal levels. However, advanced technology, mass media, and the internet are powerful information generators that flood the world with overwhelming raw information and knowledge. It is challenging to keep up with and apply them in every field perfectly productively; security management and control measures are continuously tricky, unsettling, slippery, and volatile.

Education and Democracy

Generally, every problem may have solutions or answers; however, if one cannot recognize and analyze the issues and problematic situations, how would one find the keys to the solutions and answers? Learning is a personal experience and mindful endeavor with self-social chains of give-and-take, active-reactive, leading-following, kindness-gratification, and wandering-and-discovery behaviors. Infants and children are innocent and have vulnerable minds with limited capacity to take in and comprehend information and challenges. Fluence in information and event interpretations requires adequate intellectual development, maturity, and time. Broadly imagine, information intake and experiences can affect personal belief systems, consequently affecting personal values, worldviews, and behaviors. Education may facilitate and enrich but does not dictate intellectual, moral, ethical, and spiritual development. The interceptions among aspiration, inspiration, motivation, courage, and intelligence from within can spark individual learning processes and interest to acquire knowledge to improve oneself and live a meaningful life. Education is a crucial enricher and connective tissue for self and societal development.

Philosophically and spiritually, humanity is humans' treasure and an indispensable part of life; humans are mutually earthbound companions whose quality relations seem continuously under construction with intermittent destructions. Self and social systems discoveries are the products of education as humans struggle to live as individuals in society through whatever they may have to deal with, including conflictual, meaningful, and valuable relations. How humans treat and value each other is the foundation of various forms of social relations, including attachment, cooperation, security, insecurity, stability, alienation, and hostility.

The inseparable linkage between democracy and humanity requires education to bridge and shed light on learning about, appreciating, applying, and preserving these divine treasures to facilitate and enrich humans' life journeys. Education may be a guardian angel of freedom, dignity, liberty, serenity, and critical awareness of being human.

Democracy may not fit every society as a one-size-fits-all outfit. The overall qualities and levels of self-societal development, intellectually, spiritually, morally, psychologically, academically, economically, politically, and legally, constitute an essential foundation for adopting democracy as an effective sociopolitical system to facilitate and enrich life's living experiences at individual and societal levels.

Interwoven self-societal developments are much more mysterious and complicated than cooking a meal, building constructions, or incredible rocket science. However, despite the out of reach for complete knowledge, they are within humans' intellectual, spiritual, and other divine capacities to learn about, live with, and evolve from them. Knowing it all is not a prerequisite to having and living a life. An ability to develop, grow, learn, think, and apply what one knows to keep oneself alive and well throughout a lifetime is the key to existence as an individual human being in natural, symbolic, and sociopolitical environments.

Based on some subjects such as biochemistry, organic-and-inorganic chemistry, physiology, genetics, and comparative anatomy, a human being is an individual life system consisting of biophysical and energy-generating subsystems that at a molecular level contain elements such as Carbon, Hydrogen, Oxygen, Nitrogen, Sulfur, Phosphorus, Calcium, Potassium, Sodium, Magnesium, Zinc, etc. The natural bonding and interactions among the elements display biophysical structures with various functions. The dynamic energy-generating complexes condense in central and peripheral nervous systems, leading to perceptions, feelings, fantastic human cognition, behaviors, and actions-reactions in real-life situations. From intangible cognition, comprehension, awareness, and desire to tangible body part movements, one may imagine the connections between intangible and tangible reality by observing the signals of being alive or existence and human life paths from pre-birth, birth, growth, development, life endurance, death, and beyond. Imagine everything in the universe connects directly or indirectly at various distances under the pulling-pushing or accepting-rejecting natural forces.

Humans need support from other humans, directly or indirectly, from personal to societal levels, to survive, develop, live, thrive, and evolve throughout a lifetime. Unfortunately, so many humans behave destructively against other humans, leading to adverse and toxic environments from various perspectives. All these reflect the overwhelming challenges against innocent and inexperienced minds to learn, prepare, and respond to the harmful fields of life living.

Education is a vehicle and tool to help humans become aware and understand the values and possible applications of democracy in a reciprocal detour to realize the essential role of education, opportunities, virtues, and other supportive remedies to live a hopeful and meaningful life. Education, democracy, humanity, compassion, and all other nurturing life ingredients may not be perfect like a magic wand. Still, they may somehow rescue and liberate humans from despair at the right place, time, and occasion. Ideally, they should be readily available as applicable human-made instruments in overcoming any challenge for acceptable or endurable outcomes personally and socially. Humans, collectively, should be able to craft and build sociopolitical systems that help raise, inspire, motivate, support, and protect humans per developmental processes.

The mutually constructive cyclical relations between humans and practical social systems are like a dynamically moving life-living wheel energized by education and clear communication, moving with time continuously from the present toward the future.

Jobs
The services for life living

Having a job is having a chance to make a living and build a bridge to the future or further steps in life. Earning an income means gaining a medium of exchange for everything one may desire and afford to live a daily life, take a vacation, be free, and be a human. Living may have an arbitrary standard, but at least it means keeping breathing and doing what one can reasonably do to exist and sustain one life in an ongoing fashion throughout one lifetime.

Defining a great job, good job, bad job, odd job, or lousy job depends on many factors, including income, benefits, skills, surrounding people, stress level, willingness to endure the experiences, convenience, quality of life, and whatever one may think and make an excuse or affirmation. Psychologically, one may reduce or translate the job burdens to be an income-producing companion of personal development with time. Personal-professional-and-societal developments may take place in unison through one same person on a life-living landscape.

While one is alive, one manifests the energy of living and being. Being alive and able with biophysical fitness, strength, intellect, knowledge, and skills suggests that one should earn a living and spend time actively living; otherwise, entropy kicks in, taking on the inertia of laziness, possibly leading to depression and life erosion. Take responsibility and blame no one; why not have an aspiration, a divinity of creation, and a passion for contribution and innovation?

Lead oneself before leading others; however, a leader may follow wisdom lights and expert advice. One may discipline the mind with good thinking and find something to do in searching for good ideas and possibilities. Job opportunities increase with personal qualifications and the ability to find or create one. Aim and focus on getting a job or creating jobs, keeping busy living, breathing in the fresh air, and sharing your blessings. There are many windows and doors to open for air and sunlight. Regardless of any sources of air and light, never forget you are the breath taker and the sunshine of your life.

Even though job creation is a duty of the government, any citizen may somehow participate in creative ideas and suggestions with relevant actions to employ or create jobs for oneself and others. Small businesses are motivating tools for job creation and viable economic stimulation. No one can do everything for everyone anywhere, all the time, neither the government nor citizens. Proper navigation and alignment of intelligence, passion, effective communication, and respectful relations may help bring out the best in everyone, including leadership, motivation, and practical actions from personal to governmental and societal levels. Consequently, job creation can happen along the lines of human relations. However, human abuses and exploitations are not job creation but crimes against humans and humanity.

Many urgent, complex, and challenging issues demand governments worldwide to take practical actions promptly, such as climate changes, environmental protections, terrorism, war, food-chain interruptions, human trafficking, competitive economy, inflation-recession, local-to-international conflicts, political threats, diseases, etc. Advanced technology is a massive field of jobs that can align with and increase job creation in many other areas of human needs from local to global scales. Nevertheless, we should be grateful to all dedicated experts and workers in every field who work relentlessly with compassion to contribute to the betterment of humans, humanity, and societies. Keeping oneself busy with decent activities may be a brilliant way to live, be awakened, wise, happy, and never forget to be a valuable member of society.

Bumpy Roads

Many people dream of success, and the best outcomes for their thrives in life. Life unfolds with what one can and cannot do throughout a lifetime. Mind and brain may work together during the lifetime; however, personal beliefs often lead to behaviors and actions. Eventually, someone may realize the reality that may not be the same as in the imagination or the chime of their dreams. Do not scream! Be calm and peaceful. Living life is often like walking on a gymnastic balance beam, hoping for a perfect theme and the best landing scene.

Regardless of universal or personal meanings of success, in real life, in mass media, or on a TV or cellphone screen, success is an elusive marker of a life journey under the sky that can provide sunny, dark, rainy, or stormy days or nights. Whatever it may be, keep busy living and doing your best. Do not be fearful; instead, despite the difficulty and uncertainty, stay calm, appreciate, encourage, and be respectful to the people who try to do their best (including yourself). Evolve constructively forward while beware of the earth-bound gravity and negativity of hidden prejudice and jealousy. Choose humanity over bigotry, liberate your mind-body-and-spirits, and never stop doing your best. Life is a journey forward with time; treating oneself and others respectfully with compassion is not too challenging or impossible. It is not a bad idea to yearn for civil personal conduct and civil society altogether.

Natural and social environments may powerfully influence many things, including human minds. Do not waste time debating; you are the only one who can be yourself and comfortable under your skin. Chin up; knowing right or wrong may be as good as being free. Being happy and wise in earning a living may help energize practical applications of knowledge in providing professional services and dealing with challenges in any life scene and workplace.

Be free to enlarge your mind and expand caring spirits, as no one can inhibit such aspiration except yourself. Nevertheless, we are all human beings. In any case, do not feel helpless, fearful, or jealous, but be generous, inspired, happy, and cheerful when perceiving anyone's success and happiness. Imagine an accumulation of everyone's success as a social success that may benefit everyone. Other people's success does not mean your failure or any blockage of a journey to reach yours. March on for your success while earning a living as you are its soul, crucial component, and the leader of your best.

Confidence and focus on doing one's job are not the same as being proud. Based on developmental perspectives, do not underestimate or judge the quality of any human's mind; discipline yours. Kindness and compassion are intrinsic valuable qualifications of healthcare and public service-related professionals. Laziness and disrespect issues can arise and infest workplace politics if people get trapped in a perceived elusive identity and do not realize the importance of humanity, social contributions, and compassion.

Remember, doing one best may be the best formula for success. Here and now, or at any moment, one can always try to do one best and realize the incredible freedom from within. When you have time, bless yourself with your very best.

In unknown, complex, and ambiguous situations, blaming and complaining are not solutions; resolving ideas may arise by evaluating the systems, problems, policies, processes, time, and organizational workflows. A disciplined mind is a shining quality of the pro. Ho! Ho! Ho! Yes or no, Causes-and-Effects is an invincible theory of consequential reality. Let humanity and democracy be forever blessing facilitators of humans' live-and-work journeys.

Do not get mixed up about compassionate life vision, good intentions, confidence, and work ethics with self-centered pride. Being mindful of doing anything is a kind of self-discipline. Anyone may enlarge one's mind and expand caring spirits on any bumpy road of a life journey. One is the gatekeeper of one mind, especially when dealing with dire situations or challenging conditions. Freedom and other components of democracy implicitly inspire, facilitate, and enrich human-and-societal developments. The competent, ready, and willing people mean a capable society; the rest may delay social progress, get trapped or lost in the confusion of popular worldly self-social identities, and not quite ready to join the progress.

At an individual level, it seems too heavy or impossible for the competent to lift, rescue, or help the lost. Socially, however, hope, humanity, and democracy may provide a divine avenue and shed some light that awakens and invites everyone to keep trying to move forward in the right direction by doing the right things. Everyone has to grow through whatever life may bring. Bumpy roads may keep one alert, careful, and mindful to work and live safely in harmony with sociopolitical reality.

Advanced technologies help improve access to and clarity of relevant information and knowledge for humans to help humans directly or indirectly in the world of irregular, uneven, unpredictable, and complex self-and-societal development. Collective human spirits and intelligence may enable humans to travel over life bumpy roads toward worthwhile or divine destinations. Whatever life may bring, persevere, do not hesitate to keep your mind open to learning, and be ready to welcome good vibes and wisdom light. Be delighted to bless yourself and others with love, kindness, compassion, calmness, human best, and peace.

Vision and Commitment

Imagine a life journey in the natural and human-made world. How, when, where, and why do humans come together to live and thrive for well-being while they may suffer in the battle of their conflicts of difference? These constitute collective dots of social events in the displays of interwoven natural changes and human-and-societal development processes. Natural, social, and symbolic environments generate endless challenges for humans to deal with individually as persons and collectively as communities at various levels, locally to globally, throughout life passages and human histories. Intellectual developments are the leading lights for life endurance, comprehension of reality, and ultimate self-actualization.

Changes always happen no matter what we do or do not do anything, as moving time indicates all kinds of changes; time and changes are mutual indicators of each other. We may not know or feel all of what is happening near or far, whatever they are, but some things are changing. However, it is important to acknowledge changes related to personal life-living, including natural changes in humans' biophysical bodies, minds, spirits, growth, development, and aging pathways. All changes coincide with the infinite transformation of the energy of living and being along and beyond the end of a lifetime. Imagine life must have great values and meanings to discover as one grows up and learns about life. Good intention, aspiration, and ambition inspire actions for something worthwhile.

One way to be a human is to keep oneself busy with good thinking and balancing work with life-living. The vision of achievable goals and purposes combined with a commitment to actions may intensify the determination to do one best, aiming forward with high hope and time. Anxiety or worries can tamper cognition, delay life progress, and waste valuable time. Learning to put things in perspective, prioritize and archive challenging issues in order of available solutions may help one regain control of powerful emotion for good deed deliberation.

One needs to acquire discipline, and the habit of the character one aspires to be. Success may have descriptive criteria as achievement markers according to the one who thrives on gaining it. At any moment, however, no instant success is available on sale anywhere. It is an earnest endeavor requiring aspiration, dedication, perseverance, viable knowledge, vision, and skills ultimately applicable to human well-being. Success is a marker or label of a meaningful and valuable deed, not a guarantee for happiness or a destination; it requires effort, discipline, determination, focus, persistence, and perseverance during life endurance.

Being a human, if one does not value human lives and humanity, one devalues one's own life. Moment by moment, day by day, week by week, month by month, and year by year, life's values and meanings may become more apparent as the reality of life unfolds with time. Vision and commitment may help one set a stage of self-discipline with high focus and resolution to eventually overcome the gravity of distraction and discover life's actual values and meanings. Vision and commitment toward meaningful and useful goals with humanitarian purposes may lead to success once or in a sequence, like a cascade of remarkable achievements and miracles of life.

Anyone may be alone sometimes and discover solitudes through cognition and soul-searching actions. The privacy of life living and being is not lonely; relativity and interactions are not intimidation. However, human interdependence, decent society, humanity, and functional social systems are parts of a meaningful life. No one can succeed alone in isolation, as one cannot provide everything for oneself to live a remarkable life. Humans depend on many factors and many other humans for life success and blessings along the highway of the past, present, and hopeful future.

Solitudes and Social Integration

Naturally, one was born to live a given life; the biophysical body and life experiences may be a designer tool or vehicle to find one soul and various meanings or purposes of life. From an insightful perspective, one may view a life journey as a dynamic living system displaying personal growth, development, and changes with soul energy manifestation, transformation, and refinery. Self-preserving instincts, natural biophysical functions, patterns of life directions, and birth-living-and-death events reflect the virtual equality of gravity-and-mortality-bound human beings.

The variety of human typical and uncertain life paths may reveal during the events encompassing birth, thriving to live, and doing one best daily until death. There is no inborn preprinted manual accompanying newborn delivery or automatically revealing instructions along the life path for one to do the right things at any time to be a flawlessly perfect human. All these "knowing how" mysteries or secrets are in the context of unstoppable natural energy manifestation-transformation processes and forces open for learning and discoveries. The nature and biological processes always accompany and surround humans, regardless of anyone's awareness, belief, or attention. Logics, cognition, imagination, experiences, analytical skill, knowledge, and intelligence may help bring humans closer to powerfully dynamic answers to life-living questions in a continuously changing world, naturally, socially, spiritually, educationally, economically, politically, etc.

Everyone should be free to think and have a chance to learn to live a given life at one best in respectful manners, not harmful to self or others. An ideal fusion between the inborn and acquired capacity to live a decent life may manifest in human intellectual development individually as a person and collectively as a society. Moving beyond the barriers of the differences among humans, collective intelligence and cooperation are significant contributions to help humans overcome the challenges against humanity, democracy, and humans.

The discoveries about self and others and life-related values are products of human perceptions, interactions, education, and self-societal development. Biophysical identities, including sizes, heights, colors, and other bodily displays, help humans physically identify and find each other. However, the endless ramifications of identity issues become problematic in social organizations, communication, various perspectives of personal and social values, competition for resources and power, security-insecurity concerns, politics, etc.

Life is about living, being, learning, developing, and becoming. Living large is one way to embrace self and others with a quality mind and the light of humanity. The difference does not mean or guarantee to be better or worse than, superior or inferior to one another, high or low, happy or sad, etc. No one can forever escape from the gravity and events of biophysical changes or impermanence under the natural processes of birth, being alive, living, thriving, sick, aging, and dying. Most of all, no one can confirm or deny if these indicate a perpetual-cyclical sequence of life, qualifying human development, and a part of the soul energy refinery processes.

Self-awareness, belief evaluation, and experience assessment in isolation or Solitude may help one improve self-discipline and Social Integration meaningfully. Life valuation and social responsibilities require a high level of intellectual, moral, ethical, and spiritual development that may eventually lead to comprehension of the virtual equality of life in self-societal developmental processes. It may make sense to imagine the purposes and chances to be here on earth to live, develop, and transform in association with a soul energy refinery process. Based on the concept of energy transformation, imagine. improving the grade of soul energy may correspondingly improve human character and qualifications of becoming decently autonomous. Self-proclaim to be any powerful entity or a chosen figure of power by unprovable intangible forces to cause harm, chaos, or adversely affect other humans' lives is a dangerous, outdated idea and a self-misperception or personal propaganda for self-promotion to act upon personal will, interest, and immaturity

One may review the relations between leaders and ordinary fellow human beings in a sociopolitical context and Solitude of justice. Leadership is for humans to lead and serve humans in respectable manners. In perseverance for the stability and civility of human societies, it is imperative to have transparency, check-and-balance mechanisms, and continuous improvement disciplines in sociopolitical systems, including provisions for the limitation of undue opportunities to solicit and acquire the social-psychological power to manipulate others and navigate resources for personal gain, satisfaction, and dominations. Humans play various roles in initiating and orchestrating the contents, functions, and mechanics of social systems' invention. Sociopolitical systems that lead to human exploitation and suffering are like debilitating diseases affecting humans and social stability.

Comprehension of the human intellectual developmental process is a key to sociopolitical system improvement, not a chance to exploit human innocence, spirit, and honesty. Advancing artificial intelligence should help humans acquire advanced intelligence to the extent that most humans know better about being a part of and participate more effectively in sociopolitical systems development, applications, and improvement. Solitude is where one may find oneself and one soul while disciplining the mind and persevering in doing one best.

In addition to education and training, Solitudes may provide a chance and a peaceful moment to improve personal cognition and Social Integration. Solitude, Solitude, yes, Solitude is available for anyone to cultivate, refine, and verify personal beliefs to live a meaningful-hopeful life. Life is a gift given to us by the miracle of birth and a life journey we must take; Solitude is a gift we may create for ourselves from within on the foundation of mindfulness and self-discipline. Life with Solitudes is a beautiful life with divine light shining for one to master the journey autonomously. Social Integration is an inevitable scenario and an essential part of a life journey to live exceptionally and be one best.

Collective Advancing Intelligence

Intelligence is a critical quality humans need to live as best as they can in a world of diverse challenges. One may learn and comprehend human intelligence by observing human behaviors from childhood to old age as one has to go through the developmental process like everyone else. Divine intelligence may refer constructively to an ability to take actions necessary for surviving, living, and achieving something respectable-and-worthwhile without harming oneself or others. In contrast, harmful intelligence may refer to fierce, cunning, or deceitful intelligence without regard for others' life and wellbeing. Intelligence manifests brain function in learning, analyzing, synthesizing, and applying information, knowledge, skills, and everything one may have for personally satisfying results, safety, and stability. If those personally satisfying results include the safety and welfare of others, they are a blessing of divine intelligence. However, intelligence in action leads to more interest, observation, and discoveries of more detailed, more profound, broader intelligence characterized by the quality of the driving forces, underlining values, or defining factors such as emotional intelligence, moral intelligence, ethical intelligence, situational intelligence, spiritual intelligence, academic intelligence, artificial intelligence, practical intelligence, central intelligence, peripheral intelligence, extraordinary intelligence, visionary intelligence, intuitive intelligence, social intelligence, political intelligence, crisis intelligence, diplomatic intelligence, and so on. New ideas and discoveries may result from evolving intelligence, which becomes advanced intelligence. Eventually, the combination of all intelligence in an uplifting forward dynamic with time and continuous improvement of anything for the betterment of humans, humanity, and democracy may become adaptive intelligence, continuously advancing intelligence, and practical operational intelligence.

Regardless of its description, intelligence results from personal intellectual development associated with social and natural changes. Some humans may have advanced collective intelligence with social-systems-and-human-behavior management skills suitable to be leaders. However, no concrete wall exists to confine the human mind and imagination. Effective provisional guarding systems for sociopolitical leaders are necessary to prevent power abuse while facilitating their job performances to better humans, humanity, local-and-world communities, social and natural environments, and harmony for peace. Sociopolitical systems are social instruments created by humans in human-and-societal developmental processes. Humans can develop sophisticated vehicles for journeys to many places, including the moon and Mars. Why not continuously improve, preserve, and defend humanity and democracy through collective intelligence and cooperation? Where, when, and how can they take place? Minds, brains, facts, relevant information, effective communication, fact verification, collaboration, and transparency are fundamental ingredients for humans to make them happen and continue to happen fruitfully. Let's do it like breathing in fresh air while living life and mindfully passing on ideas, discipline, and responsibilities to future generations. The synchronicity of human excellence reflects the autonomy of human intelligence and the continuity of the species' existence.

Spread Love, Spread Natural Power

Love, comfort, safety, security, trust, and hope are beautiful feelings supposedly available in a home environment and a divine society. Humans behave and relate to others diversely under natural and sociopolitical circumstances or situations. Generally, beliefs and values play crucial roles in human behaviors and social integration; education can improve knowledge, living skills, job qualifications, and human relations. Unfortunately, mental and psychological conditions caused by many factors such as heredity, abuse, accidents, traumatic experiences, deception per lies, misleading, and misinformation can affect perception, cognition, values, beliefs, personal convictions, attitudes, and behaviors. More or less love may help craft and improve those qualifications per support, advocacy, encouragement, education, and delivery of facts or valid information. Facts and accurate information lead to clearer perceptions, comprehension, differentiation between right and wrong, true or false, and how to decently get along with others.

Love leads to and expands empathy, compassion, and commitment to protecting and supporting loved ones in any situation. Intellectual developments happen in a life-living context that shapes thinking styles, beliefs, values, and attitudes. However, information, messages, communications, mass media, commercial ads, political propaganda, and advanced technologies can affect perceptions and thought processes through repetition, impression, and compelling psychological persuasion. Love drives caring minds to find ways to protect their loved ones from toxic information and misinformation so they can live life wisely, safely, and fruitfully. Love is a positive volunteer emotion residing within a merciful and lovely mind. Commitment and discipline fortify love. Love is a silent, powerful motivator for behaviors and decision-making. Love can do many incredible things, and behavioral science may help highlight those in broader and deeper dimensions.

Parental love gave me soul energy, strength, and the light of life; receiving and giving love are dual blessings. I love Mother Theresa's tenacity to serve humans and humanity with great love per a resonating channel of commitment to society and personal discipline guided by ethical and moral values. Love carries loyalty, responsibility, and respect, yielding affection, compassion, kindness, patience, and time to review, learn, and understand human behaviors. Love is an unexhaustive spiritual asset of a giver and powerful delightful energy for the receiver. True love refreshes the soul, fueling courage, and is a fortifier of the spirits and a receptacle of trust.

A discussion about love is like a pep talk that may not yield anything objectively immediately. However, if everyone learns to love oneself and others and continues navigating loving emotion without discrimination, some days someone may have an extraordinary, powerful mind to wipe out hate from within. Eventually, the world will be a better place. Love may be powerful enough to seek caution, intelligence, and diplomacy as remedies to solve problems. Love is always affordable if one can remove defensive argumentative attitudes and illusive ego.

Most humans receive nurturing parental love; unfortunately, some miss the chance. Growing up without parental love is hard, but one may learn about love. Love can grow from the inside of human minds, and spreading love may mean distributing power and affording one to be kind. The power of love may trigger compassion and enhance motivation to live life meaningfully. Beware; however, humans may get lost with or without love. Intellect is a companion of love to keep the mind in balance and wide open for divine energy drive to be one best.

Love is more than just a wonderful thing. It is immeasurable, refreshing, powerful, and available from within. Feel free to agree or disagree with the opinions about love; a caring mind is happy and calm when no one hurts anyone, and everyone lives decently and peacefully. One may distribute lots of love to everyone through prayers and best wishes. Love may make one feel relevant and enjoy the best of personal dimensions. Every life is precious, and one may envision the excellent light inside to guide one life. The world is so big, and there are plenty of spaces to live and be oneself; it is possible to live decently and safely without hurting anyone. Let the divine lights shine for one to be kind and wise while striving to do one best.

In many situations, it seems very hard or impossible to be happy alone; thrive, keep trying a little bit at a time with moving time. Time may be a magical vehicle to carry anyone to wherever one may want to be if one does not let evils distract and pull one off the divine highways on any day of one life. Eventually, possibilities will appear; one may have the power of love enough to have the aspiration and courage to develop, endure, persevere, and foster personal success. Remember, if one cannot jump or leap so high, one can always make a move, one little step at a time, with divine efforts to climb higher and higher on the mountain of inevitable challenges. Eventually, one may reach the highest pivotal point of life, conquering challenges and seeing the clearer panoramic view of continuously unfolding reality. Then, one has earned the most remarkable success through one firm commitment to being the best of oneself. There, one gets the blessing of excellence and uniqueness of one best.

Love is not limited to only for lovers, relatives, friends, or immediate family members. Humans may spread love to themselves and others through humanity and any vehicle of divinity. Naturally, one may realize the existence of love when one learns to love oneself and extend the love to others. One may cultivate, enrich, and expand the love from the inside by enlarging the mind and spirit. Feel free to bless yourself and others with love. Yes! You can. Love is kind; love enriches the wisdom of life. Be free to love, be loved, and appreciate love. Many people may want to know the real meaning of love and silently demand, "Tell me what LOVE is."

Well! Love is a Lift Of Visionary Excellence, a Load Of Vital Energy, a Land Of Virtuous Elegance, a Lane Of Vibrant Eternity, a Lead Of Visionary Equation, and the Light On Victorious Elevation, Let Outstanding Vibes Evolve. True love is pure, precious, powerful, and wonderful to give and receive.

Freedom, Humanity, and Energy of Living

The natural linkage of existing and living while developing is an incredible theme of being a human at any age, social status, and location in the real world. Human relations reflect the dynamic flows and manifestations of living energy. Keeping oneself busy with healthy activities is a key to living. Sunshine and the light of freedom awaken humans through the perspectives of vision, cognition, and motions for learning and living. Ka-ching, Ka-ching, living energy is free to cultivate and enrich oneself joyfully. Do not mind where it may originate from. Imagine and feel it as it flows through active, strong, resilient, courageous, hopeful, and purposeful minds. It is wise, nurturing, healthy, and delightful to selectively navigate, filter, and retain the good vibes during thriving to live a given life.

Imagine, bit by bit; humanity serves as an all-purpose remedy and instrument to foster as well as enrich human relations in a divinely refreshing manner. Investing in humanity and society is worthwhile, healthy, visionary, and wise, even though realizing and measuring success is challenging. Human behaviors affect their relationship reciprocally with complexity and mysteries. How do humans develop viable social systems that favor coexistence, quality living, hope, bringing out human best, and progress? No perfect sociopolitical system exists to serve or indulge humans romantically and limitlessly. Democracy seems to be the most valuable imperfect system to seek and bring out people's best.

Human behaviors may be complex displays of the mysterious life living energy from the inside out. However, humans need food, shelter, exchange currencies, external energy sources, and other essential components for living various lifestyles. These imply that everything may relatively mingle through the seamless channels of energy flow and sparkling interceptions. Superficial identities and changes in everything are displays of energy flow from stable orders, transitional positions, and chaos in full circles of its potential. Energy comprehension and marvelous microwave technology may lead to more human magical discoveries.

Freedom and humanity are powerful virtues that may make anyone feel so good and blessed to be a human. How can humans move past the alienating differences and insecurities to find a sacred common ground for alignments of our best to lead, facilitate, and enrich our lives wherever we are? Freedom and humanity can help humans develop and advance beyond racial prejudice and the divisive restrictions of national, cultural, or sociopolitical barriers.

Contentment and ambition are contradictory emotions helpful in doing our best from what we can learn, know, and apply while we live our lives with what we have any time, wherever we are. Based on the availability of freedom, humanity, and the synergy of working together to solve life-living problems, we may get many correct answers for any question adaptively on a life journey from the present to the future. There is plenty of evidence and stories from the past to make sense for humans never to give up hope. Per collective human intelligence with resilient minds and thriving souls, we can eventually discover solutions for any imposing problem, even though we may need a lot of time to reach a chime of best success. From cave style to high-rise buildings, walking to flying, none to abandon knowledge, continuous curiosity to endless dreams, alone or with a ready and exciting team, humans may discover and do magic beyond their best through freedom, humanity, and the energy of living.

The Impermanence of Biophysical Appearance, an Illusion of Reality

Understanding human behaviors, information analysis, materialism, discontent, spirituality, and all kinds of events one may encounter in daily life is crucial for adapting to, living in, and evolving from one moment to another with the lifting positivity over the gravity of opposing forces. Continuous dynamic processes of changes, human behaviors, sociopolitical and natural events, diverse identities, languages, and symbolic avenues of communication *generate* infinite complex challenges to being human and living a given life.

How can humans identify and solve confronting problems, deal with changes, and develop constructively without adversely affecting others? The dynamic of reality happens naturally in unison, along with the consequential processes of changes, which continue with time. Simplifying everything in personally understandable configurations results from an individual style of thinking and viewing the world one may live in; it is a personal worldview.

Genetics, cognition, mobility, communications, learning ability, knowledge, skills, locations, social connections, and environments significantly affect the quality of life and individual uniqueness or overall identity. Unfortunately, not everyone can get quality education, support, and inspiring-motivating guidance; however, applying what one knows effectively is a gate opener to the pathway for survival and success. Predicament and troubles dominate when personal best is not enough to overcome the flaw of unfolding fate, resulting in misery and suffering. However, hope and possibility may still exist within the mind and soul that own indomitable will to be free with the spirit of liberty to go on beyond the physical capacity.

Human biophysical structures change to a certain extent under internal and external influences on developmental processes that only last for a lifetime. Regardless of beliefs, prayers, power, wealth, or wishes, no one can choose, dictate, and design the life one may be born into, but one may strive to live the given life as best as possible. Nature is so mysterious and powerful beyond human control. However, per observations, imagination, and experiences of human personal-social-and-natural phenomena of life from pre-birth, birth, growth, development, illness, aging, and death, life is an impermanent form of energy manifestation, the dynamic of energy of living and being.

Under the incredible mysteries of nature involving changes, energy, and the laws of thermodynamics, death is not the end of the soul journey and energy transformation. Imagine human souls may be under a common natural pathway of changes manifesting multiple forms of appearances, such as diverse races in perpetual life cycles or patterns of being. The perceptions and feelings coincide with the body and mind when one is alive in each life biophysical body. These are the foundations of personal identity in alignment with social essence.

An ability to acquire information, help, and guidance fruitfully may lead to personal strategic endurance to reach goals consecutively throughout life. How to be safe and live well is a baseline of personal life endeavors. Physical or biophysical forms of nonliving and living things are stagnant and immobile without active energy and dynamic interactions. Interactive processes are consequential and timely reflective. Humans have feelings, cognition, emotion, and judgment; however, confusion and miscalculation of actions-reactions can lead to suffering and disappointment. Self-management skills mentally, psychologically, intellectually, and spiritually are necessary for self-empowerment to live a decent life and fearlessly become the autonomous leader of one soul's journey.

Reality is infinite, and so is the continuity of changes. Trying to control the uncontrollable wastes mind, energy, and time, like unconsciously approaching a failure of imagination and delusions. Recognition and comprehension of the personal dimension of reality as a part of the wholeness of infinite reality is the key to surviving and adapting more efficiently than trying to acquire or change everything to satisfy personal desire, void of mindfulness and self-discipline.

Lost and Found In Uneven Development

A comparison of humans to human look-alike animals leads to a question about how humans could develop from the stage of insignificant or negligible apes to be brilliant, decent humans or fall short and become troublemakers or pathetic social leaders. How could humans have superior capacities to chimpanzees, monkeys, or other ape species? Knowing or developing verifiable, complete answers for the whole truth is impossible. However, referring to many knowledge areas of science and nonscience, including geography, archeology, psychology, biology, chemistry, physics, zoology, sociology, mythology, arts, spirits, etc., the concepts about energy manifestation and transformation, consequential changes over time, and evolution point to the directions and possibilities involving uncountable or billion years of chronological changes and developments. The apparent human dominance over chimpanzees, monkeys, or other animals on earth is the overall display of genetic expressions, biophysical appearances, and the products of brain functions such as cognition, creativity, languages, innovation, construction, communication, social organization, culture, belief systems, religions, etc. Humans are superior and much more advanced than animals in almost every aspect except the intangible wonder, mind-driven behaviors, social relations, and spiritual capacity because they may be observable or inferable but immeasurable. We do not know the quality of the mind until we experience expressive behaviors. Insecurity and fear lead to an attempt to identify the threats or the sources of threats to neutralize or escape from them. Superficial identities catch the visual perception and imprint the memory of experiences from human behaviors.

Generalizing external identities with behaviors invokes an erroneous alienation and discrimination against other humans; not every human is the same regarding the wholeness of life and being. Behaviors, developmental potential, and personal-social environments are important fate-unfolding factors. The interface between genetic expression and environments leads to development, growth, and changes in various perspectives throughout an individual lifetime. Human developmental processes may be uneven individually at a personal level and collectively at social levels. Individually, one may get better or worse, as do the trends of human herds or society.

Misperception makes one get lost in miscomprehension of self and others until experiences and education facilitate brain functional development to a competent level to overcome cognitive challenges. One may need time to find oneself with clarity of thoughts alone or with the assistance of intellectual lights shining from others. Humans may get lost but eventually discover each other in social flows of uneven development if they adopt a positive attitude and try to overcome the fear of differences, mysteries, and disparities. We are here on earth with life; should we discover what it means? Our important natural assignment on the eventful life journey may be to guard ourselves against either doing evil, being the victims of evil acts, or both.

Comfort, security, and hope are primary motives for mutual respect, togetherness, and social formation. Embrace the goodness of life, reject what is wrong, and adopt what is right; in any situation, it's wise to keep calm and try to find the bright side of life. When humans work together to save lives, we may witness the miracle and power of compassion and gratification that come from the inside of the human mind,

No one lives forever. Whatever it is, focusing on living life is wise and practical; in a lifetime, one may learn about the incredible meanings, purposes, and values of life as a human being. Moreover, someone may discover new ideas and inventions in favor of quality of life, longevity, and peaceful coexistence. Pray for everyone to have a long and wonderful life with empathy, love, kindness, and compassion. Someone may cultivate and harvest the truth along the phenomena of changes and appreciate the life of oneself and other humans who may be friends or strangers.

Social identities, Sociopolitical environments, and Mental health

A chance to have a life is precious and excellent if one is lucky enough to have everything to facilitate personal development, life living, and autonomy. However, it is questionable for a life with many challenges, including the hostility of human ignorance, mysteries, misery, getting lost with no direction, hopelessness, and confusion; these are very heavy for a little angel or a newborn to carry on. From birth, childhood, youth, and adulthood, knowing and finding freedom, liberty, dignity, justice, and hope may be challenging or out of reach when one is on the roads of human interactions with plenty of abuse, adverse consequences, and misguided directions. The detrimental challenges may flip life upside down and push one into the dark side of life, robbing the chance to find life's meanings, values, and guiding light.

Humans may give humans caring messages and advocacy to inspire, motivate, and encourage individual or group efforts to overcome relentless challenges. Ensuring the availability of living space for one to exist and develop to be an exceptional human being is precious for those at the crossroads of confusion, uncertainty, vulnerability, immaturity, and loneliness. Life may be cruel, ruthless, unfair, and filled with despair in a crisis or hostile environment. It is pivotal to have a chance to survive, thrive, and find education to help open a gate of life with intellectual light to carry on. Positive attitudes and education may turn on and enhance the light of life and energy of living for one to persevere with an evolution from fear, insecurity, nothingness, many threats, and hopelessness.

A vulnerable mind, violent social environments, and exposure to misinformation and deception are severe challenges to the individual life coping ability. One inevitably faces fear, confusion, insecurity, and difficulty in filtering and applying the information to make decently relevant decisions. Social identities affect self-perception and social integration; when one needs help, it is an instinct to seek help and hope. However, depending on the urgency and severity of the problems, getting help requires proper usage of languages, communication skills, awareness of the laws, environment, and symbolic comprehension, which may lead to more confusion, frustration, and mental health crises. Sociopolitical systems powerfully influence the human minds and life-living landscape. An isolated individual is more vulnerable to predicaments or dangers than one in an affluent and morally competent society. Such a society may facilitate effective communication, healthcare services, and social support systems per availability and continuous improvement of affordable services corresponding to human needs.

Instant comfort, assurance, security, strength, support, and direction for recovery from frightening experiences towards renewing and reentry into the theme of possibilities and accessible resources are life essential. Unfortunately, help automation may not be possible, and an automatic help machine is unavailable. Most of the time, it is hard to find immediate help, as everyone is struggling for one life in the climate of a scary and care deficiency society. Human abuse, oppression, and exploitation are social diseases caused by humans against humans and humanity. Slavery, crime, and war are tragedies that include human abuse, oppression, exploitation, and destruction of life.

Plenty of life-threatening events happen continuously, naturally, and socially. However, one should not and cannot live with fear, or otherwise, it may be the same as one has no life. As one cannot escape from fear, one must transform the fear into fuel for perseverance and endurance with evolution to conquer the challenges. Human development, generally and personally, mingles with social development at large. Despite enduring efforts, possibilities, and positivity, life may still be challenging, complicated, or confusing. How should we strive to do our best in the living process? Human interactions interface with social systems functions, manifesting the waves of lives and social events flowing continuously in existential cascades until interruptive imbalances trigger changes connectively to new dynamics of lives and social events. Humans have a limited lifetime; however, humanity and democracy may

represent social instrumental concepts for people to apply, improve, modify, polish, and pass on from generation to generation. They can exist and continue to advance with human and societal developmental processes beyond humans' lifetime; they are powerful, hopeful gifts from humans to humans and society.

Changes and time coexist, enlisting social paradigm shifts into reality. Humans may do their best to elevate the paradigm while it is shifting. "I cannot do anything, or We cannot do anything" is a haunting or paralyzing phrase that can halt or compromise human and social progress for a long time.

Afterall, unfortunately, people's mental health crises may be critical signals of sociopolitical systems malfunction, corruptions, injustice, discrimination, abuses, human right violation, deterioration of morality, and other pathetic social or political influences.

Social MUD Flow Theory

Life is precious. Humanity and democracy are human-made philosophies or ideologies for humans to appreciate a chance at life, learn to live, develop toward decency, and comprehend the values and meanings of being human and life. It is impossible to construct a perfect social theory to cover and explain the wholeness of human nature, life, mind, behaviors, experiences, and future in the natural and human-made world. Some people may know a lot and can do many things. Interestingly, based on the limitation of perception and biophysical capacities, we do not and cannot know everything. Of course, nobody can do everything and be everywhere simultaneously.

Nevertheless, we may try to learn and do our best from what we know and what we have. This theory evolved from a human curiosity, vision, and attempts to understand natural-personal-social identities and the social flow of human behaviors that affect personal development and social integration on an unfolding life journey, thereby affecting societal development. It is only a narrative relative and open-ended theory, a little dot of the light for life comprehension.

Mind, body, soul, spirit, and intellect are related energy compartmental structures of life, the form and formless components of one same person. Imagine the flow of intangible energy; what affects one will affect all in consequential unquantifiable processes and outcomes of interactive self-societal development on earth.

Generally, family and home environment should be initial grounds for human development. With a careful revision of an early stage of life, childhood, and adulthood, one may realize that love, kindness, comfort, security, and hope are fundamental ingredients that attract simple social formation beginning at home. It may expand through the bridges of virtues, human connections, and communication to broader, deeper, and more complex natural and social contexts.

Many negative influences, violence, disasters, or destructive human behaviors adversely affect humans and societies repeatedly throughout human history, causing predicaments, suffering, chaos, and loss of lives along the processes of human and societal development. We should not accept them as "normal," "these things always happen," "not my problem," "nothing I can do about it," or "Oh well! It is God's will" to avoid stress and anxiety from personal-social limitations, helplessness, powerlessness, or hopelessness. Humans cause most human predicaments in addition to natural forces on the earthbound social-natural life platform. The question of how and when these will ever get better, if not fade away, demands humans to regularly pay attention, think, and search for answers in keeping up with or ahead of challenging events or situations accompanying the unfolding reality of life. These are an unpleasant unwanted inevitability of life and being human; take them as challenges for divine evolution.

When sufficient awareness and prevention of the danger are not present ahead of the risk or threat, vulnerability may increase and lead to suffering at a tragic moment when the predator harms the victim(s) or unexpected danger strikes. There are too many incidents of human suffering to comprehend and address the details of all the cause-and-effect in isolated cases or collective chains of the eventful cascade of interactive behaviors in the context of human interactions and development. Human destructive or harmful interactions may occur suddenly or slowly, directly or indirectly, immediately detectable to forever hiding like the mystery of misery. The suffering can be physical, emotional, mental, intellectual, financial, spiritual, psychological, etc., to various extents, levels, and combinations.

Suffering at a personal level may not set any significant alarm at a legal and sociopolitical scale to cause widespread fear and concern in society, locally and globally. Without a coping strategy, one may suffer alone or with loved ones until the memories fade or the end of life. However, childhood suffering may leave a psychological wound deep in the vulnerable mind as hidden memories that eventually affect the attitude, beliefs, values, personality, psyche, moral and ethical capacity, cognition, and social integration. In addition to quality education, chains of human connections in society, such as friends, family, co-workers, leaders, followers, and many other possible social roles, may lead one to acquire a job or life position in sociopolitical systems with impactful power over many human lives. Imagine when imperfect socio-political systems without adequate safety guards against errors or failure interface with the systems role-takers such as operator, manager, commander, governor, or country's leader who has concealed or unrecognized mental illness, ethical deficiency, or moral handicaps can lead to disaster or chaos in society from local to global scales in the forms of social conflicts, crime, famine, slavery, genocide, corruption, disaster, terrorism, wars, mass destructions, etc.

MUD is the key word for this theory which refers to or suggests many possible dangers, hostile forces, risks, destructions, or predicaments that humans may contribute directly or indirectly to social systems and other humans. They may individually and collectively impact victims and society, leading self and others to sink deeper into challenging social environments like the heavy gravity of negativity against personal and societal developments. Analogically imagine humans suffer and get stuck in a pool of forcefully sticky, down-pulling mud with uncertainty to be safe and survive. Who can help? Where is the help? How may one find help? What is a life journey? What is humanity? What is it, and where can one find the effective rescuing lift of life?

Struggles, aspirations, courage, and perseverance to live and escape from the danger, burdening conditions, and down-pulling predicaments are not so simple because it is not easy to identify and manage the problem effectively and promptly. An evolution to constructively and victoriously turn a life around or reinvent oneself is critical, unfortunately, often leaning toward the impossible. One may have many questions when steering the wheel of life toward possibility and positivity. Where is personal power to take one life to another level as best as one can, like renewing, refreshing, or recovering from an unfortunate situation or condition? When one cannot rescue oneself alone, one depends on luck, chances, availability and kindness of other humans, miracles, and functional social systems.

Curiosity, aspiration, education, training, experiences, living skills, expertise, and time take humans to various markers of life's journey from childhood to adulthood and maturity. It is OK if one is decently happy and delightfully enjoys life; however, one may suffer if one falls into vulnerable or victim situations beyond self-rescuing capacity. Despite the luck of being alive, the suffering may have a long-lasting psychological impact. The struggles of living, being, behaving, and becoming may contribute to both positive and negative consequences among interactive parties on future life paths. Imagine the interception of negative impacts may create more human sufferance as linear, multidirectional, or cyclical social mudflow of humans affect humans, directly or indirectly, through the imperfection of social and natural systems and human behaviors.

There are countless human-related interactions and reciprocal influences that may lead to many possible outcomes, including flows of negative impacts or continuous social mudflow. An arbitrary list of

reciprocally interactive pairs (←→ = "interact with, influence, do something to, or mutually impact") is as follow:

Human ←→Social systems (politics, economy, cultures, etc.)

Human ←→Human,

Humans ←→Human

Humans ←→Humans

Humans ←→Natural environment

Humans ←→ Symbolic environment

Humans ←→ Sociopolitical systems

The dynamic unevenness of changes, growth, construction, destructions, and developments of every changeable thing may be an underlying factor for the imperfection of everything in the human world. Conceivably, the patterns, speeds, levels, styles, magnitudes, forms, and formlessness of life-related matters and uncertainty are clues for the complexity and difficulty of life. The MUD in Social Mud Flow Theory refers to anything, behaviors, conditions, or situations that may adversely affect humans, which may include but are not limited to the following:

Misplaced Unfortunate Deprivation	Multiple Unbearable Deprivation,
Multiple Undetectable Destructions	Major Unsustainable Damage
Major Unsolvable Deviations	Multiple unrepairable damages
Massive Undisclosed Destruction	Multifaceted Undetectable Danger
Multifaceted Undue Deterioration	Multifaceted Unaware Deception
Multiple Uncontrollable Delusion	Mind Under Degradation
Mobile Unstoppable Deception	Mobile Unstoppable Destruction
Mingled Undesirable Domination	Multiple Unlawful Drug-dealing
Mentally Unfortunate Development	Misbehave Undisciplined Directors
Many Unethical Declarations	Messy Unorganized Delegation
Maligned Unforgivable Deception	Misguided Unfortunate Direction
Misfitted Under Developments	Maligned Undiscipline Deceivers
Massive Unstoppable Disinformation	Massive Undue Deception

Misguided Unfamiliar Directions   Multiple Unaware Deterioration

Mixed Up Damages   Man-woman Unending Debate

Massive Unexpected Drug-alcohol-and-chemical abuse

Manning Unsafe Devices-or-weapons   Massive Undue Disintegration

The behavior triggering belief in the humans' vulnerable mind from childhood onward to adulthood comes from other humans of any age who can create significant delusion, brainwashing, misperception, injuries, torture, pain, and fear that undermine others' behaviors. Imagine one dot of one such event may spread sparkling chains of trouble social mudflow while no one knows anything about them. Imagine a chain of human abuse physically, sexually, psychologically, etc., and the victims suffer in silence or adopt the predator behaviors and create new chains of social mudflow on and on. The worst is when humans accept wrong as correct and cruelty as the norm, culture, or tradition. Ignorance, inadequate self-discipline, and lack of empathy and social responsibilities can trigger messy chains of social mudflow. One person or group of humans may ignite social unrest, war, or catastrophe through loopholes and inadequate systems security.

Many people may feel fearful and insecure, not knowing how to deal with their predicament and lead themselves to be silent. Silence may imply weakness, fear, anxiety, endless wait, getting lost, inability to fight back, slow struggle for the best attempt to respond, planning, or lack of courage to evolve relentlessly.

One may suffer or die alone, but no one can prevent and solve the problems of human predicaments alone. Social formations of various purposes and configurations, from families, communities, organizations, and countries, to international alliances, are promising solutions to the problems. Still, it is not enough to prevent or alleviate human suffering because the availability of intelligence, resources, connectivity, collaboration, communication, and comprehension of the truths and facts cannot completely neutralize the endless and continuously evolving challenges. On the one hand, these seem to support the claim that history always repeats itself. On the other hand, continuity of constructive innovation and evolution for the human common good is essential for the existence of the human species. Please do not take these as stress but as a blessing of best awareness to empower humans with the truth, relevant information, or facts for humanity and democracy to be the faithful companions of human progress.

Whatever it is, the autonomy of human decency and collective advancing intelligence, including natural-authentic and artificial intelligence with rapid resolutions to deal with any challenge offensively and defensively, are indispensable powerful instruments to secure the momentum of human progress.

Humanity and democracy are human-made concepts, social remedies, or philosophies with great application potential for human well-being and societal development. There is no perfect sociopolitical system to serve humans passively with a satisfaction guarantee. However, democracy is compatible with humanity; together, they can bring out the human best to serve themselves and society. Education may enrich the social-intellectual platform and connectivity of everything to increase awareness, intellect, access to facts, and collaboration to brighten human life journeys. Humans never run out of jobs or something meaningful to do at any time as long as they seek measures to serve themselves and others. Anyone may want to prevent social MUD formation, stop the flow, rescue human beings, comfort human souls, restore decency, solidify dignity, and rebuild societies.

Humans need to take responsibility to learn and realize the values of social mechanisms and systems of power-sharing with active participation to live a life and be human intelligently and exceptionally. When the social MUD flows over the vulnerable in an imperfect society, it may be very messy. How should humans empower and protect themselves when social systems and the government cannot provide perfect protection? Connections, collaboration, cooperation, alert systems, warning, education and training, adaptive legal systems, transparency, and whatever is necessary to form supplemental security systems seem promising. Leadership in the government and private sectors may be the sources for the creation and promotion of human alliance for safety and decent living in society.

We may always try to do our best with good intentions and self-discipline. It is unnecessary or impossible to be perfect or chase perfection. Relax! Let it chase us. Imperfection is an opportunity and a challenge for continuous improvement to keep up with changes. Anyone may choose to fill one's mind with good thinking and enjoy doing good deeds with humble satisfaction and happiness. Life has plenty of good choices and practical reasons; it's up to humans to find and decide to apply them.

Democracy Is A Gateway To Life

Sociopolitical systems reflect extraordinary human creativity that can yield benefits with many side effects that can impact human lives, much like the contrary of the mighty nature that can provide landscape and nutrients to live with hidden threats of earthquakes, volcano eruptions, floods, fires, and storms. People are busy earning a living, striving to live a life in any situation. No one can do everything for oneself to achieve a decent quality of life alone. Humans depend on each other's goodness to be their best. Society, political systems, and natural contexts are life platforms regardless of any value or viewpoint. Intellectual development and education increase the human potential to learn about and live a given life. An ability to learn, think and express oneself is critical for personal as well as societal development. Oppression, suppression, and exploitation of human beings are toxic to security, stability, development, and well-being from the individual to the societal levels. Democracy may not be perfect, but it is the best sociopolitical system that humans can participate in shaping and benefit from. Education, democracy, and humanity are indispensable triple gems to enrich human lives, fresh air and divine lights for living, and resources for personal and societal developments. The connectivity of virtuous qualities in humans is an essential nutrient for functional social systems. Being awakened, aware, and autonomous to function and live a decent life in society is the best gift that no money can buy. However, one may earn it through education and self-discipline with support from fellow human beings and sociopolitical systems. Democracy is a gateway to life, a meaningful life.

Summary

Security, safety, education, self-confidence, and an ability to function in society are essential components for surviving, living, and developing in the human world that offers plenty of uncertainty, hope, endless challenges, threats, and possibilities. Life is precious. It is a gift, a journey, a refinery of soul energy, often an adventure, and most blessing of all, an opportunity to learn along the journey to find its values and meanings with a bonus to be oneself. What else one may desire is in the light of wisdom and imagination.

Humans cannot succeed alone, as no one can provide all the necessities for surviving and living by oneself at all times. Social formation begins with interpersonal bridges in the form of virtues and positive emotions like love, kindness, friendship, caring, compassion, and cooperation for shared values and common good. Human interdependence is like natural social instinct with give-and-take relationships and trusts that humans may develop in different life or social circumstances. The give and take may not be equally in balance or quantifiable mathematically; however, qualitatively or spiritually, they exist seemingly like the dynamic flow of the energy of being and living.

The uniqueness of personal identities results from many known and unknown factors, locations, times, and processes that may be natural and human-made. It may be the mingling of interfaces among genetics and social and natural environments. Learning, interpersonal interactions, and recognition of the difference between self and others occur from childhood to adulthood. These human experiences reflect interwoven processes of self and societal development from a family level to more complex and extensive community levels.

An expectation or assumption about human behaviors in social relations may not be possible or accurate every time or all the time; it may need professional skills or training for sensible comprehension. Human diversity, mystery, and interception among the differences can lead to ongoing conflicts and problems socially. These obstacles require a combination of divine strength, wisdom, and indomitable will to embrace and try to comprehend the inevitable problems to prevent,

minimize, solve, and manage them in order to improve the human quality of life and peaceful coexistence. However, how humans judge and value each other reflects how they treat each other, as mind and belief influence human behaviors. The level, quality, stage, and style of human development may convincingly display in behaviors, habit, self-discipline, and ability to comprehend deeply about self and others. The social MUD flow theory is a personal effort to comprehend how human developmental pathways, behaviors, and choices may lead to the traps of predicaments and what may be the applicable prevention and solutions. Sociopolitical systems, social-natural-and-symbolic environments, and self-and-societal developments are interweaving strands of the fabrics of life and human evolution. The qualities of the people reflect the qualities of the society.

Imagine countries or nations are large social organizations supposedly for unity and harmony of quality living. There are good and bad behaviors in every society. Insecurity, immaturity, ignorance, and lack of education may lead to alienation, discrimination, and prejudice against the difference. Sociopolitical systems are human-made tools to manage and influence human behaviors to attain social order under the power of system organizations, rules, laws, regulations, and leadership. Education may provide a lot of tips to comprehend these matters.

Humanity and democracy are nourishing philosophies created by humans to bring out the human best for self-empowerment to be, live, learn, develop, and share both power and responsibilities with others for justice, civility, and social progress. Through the perspectives of changes and development, self and societal development are interwoven processes with energy manifestation and transformation vocally, physically, psychologically, politically, intellectually, etc.

Artificial intelligence (AI) allows humans to know more and learn more about anything they may be curious to learn. In the past, long before the epic of AI, human intelligence was suppressed by lack of or inadequate access to knowledge and information; only the elite groups of people had the luxury of knowing more than the unfortunate ones. It is a miracle that human intelligence led to the discovery of AI, which plays a significant leading role in the reciprocal propelling of changes and progress of everything it can touch. The captivating brilliance of AI demands humans to reevaluate the values, meanings, and directions of human and societal development from a personal level to a global level. Rapid changes in everything resulting

from AI compel humans to adapt and evolve to coexist with the rapidly incredible changes in everything.

Whatever it is, the autonomy of human decency and collective advancing intelligence, including natural-authentic and artificial intelligence with instantaneous resolute actions to deal with any challenge offensively and defensively, are indispensable powerful instruments to secure the momentum of human progress.

Beginning from little pencil dots of hand-drawn mandalas to mind-made life, actively living by doing one best to take care of oneself in alignment with fellow human beings, humanity, democracy, and social progress is possible compared to countless accumulation of tiny dots of water that can become an ocean. Being oneself is excellent. However, realizing that one is a part of society locally and globally is imperative and may make a lot of difference in attitude and human relations.

All of the above is a prayer in a fusion language of art, love, simplicity, gratification, best wishes, and hope for humans, humanity, and democracy to synergistically, meaningfully, and fruitfully function for the peaceful coexistence of the human species. Enjoy the beauty and let the imperfection of this book stimulate new and practical ideas for human progress in harmony with time.

About the Author

The author is a mother, grandmother, pharmacist, and artist who has struggled through life's challenges similarly to so many of us, human beings, thriving to live with hope and perseverance. The challenges served as imposing lessons of various kinds, including poverty, lack of opportunity and resources, competition, discrimination, deception, prejudice, disrespect, bullying, harassment, and many other unpleasant treatments from some people within the social context of her life journey. However, with a resilient and creative mind, she realized that she could not change the people like crafting a statue since everyone has to endure one's life journey and behave according to individual capacity and developmental level. Moreover, she realized that the relations between human development and societal development are complex and very interesting. What should I do? and what can I do? are her routine questions. She is interested in natural circular patterns of cause-and-effect sequential processes applicable to solving problems or dealing with challenges. She believes that we, humans, can contribute more to help make the process of living a human life more sustainable and perhaps more delightful to endure. Freedom to think and intellectual development are essential and inseparable for a meaningful life. Intellectual expressions can be done in various fashions, such as writing, making a speech, playing musical instruments, singing, dancing, drawing, painting, etc. Overall, collective self-expression throughout one's life trajectory exhibits itself as an individualized art of living. One may bring one's best any moment during one's lifetime without a prerequisite of anyone else's permission and validation. She values life, quality of life, human decency, spirits, intelligence, mutual respect, empathy, and altruism, leading herself onto the platform of philosophy, arts, and humanity. A deeper review of social events worldwide demanded that embracing life, humanity, and diversity is essential for humans to work together for the common good, peaceful coexistence, progress, and human civilization. The collective spirit of democracy and humanity resides within her prayer for a better world.